Color & Learn Easy GERMAN PHRASES FOR KIDS

Roz Fulcher

Ich liebe Dich.
ikh **lee**-beh dich

Dover Public[...]
Mineola, [...]

This handy book will have you speaking German in no time! More than sixty illustrated pages include commonly used words and phrases in both German and English. Below each German word or phrase you'll find its pronunciation. A syllable that is **boldfaced** should be stressed.

Whether it's just for fun, for travel, or to have a conversation with a friend or relative, you'll find out how to talk about the weather, tell what you'd like at mealtime, and many other helpful phrases—and you can color while you learn!

Copyright

Copyright © 2015 by Dover Publications, Inc.
All rights reserved.

Bibliographical Note

Color & Learn Easy German Phrases for Kids is a new work,
first published by Dover Publications, Inc., in 2015.

International Standard Book Number

ISBN-13: 978-0-486-80360-9
ISBN-10: 0-486-80360-0

Manufactured in the United States by RR Donnelley
80360001   2015
www.doverpublications.com

Good morning.

Hello.   Good-bye.

2

See you later.

3

What's your name?

My name is _____.

Das ist
dahss isst

1. meine Mutter
my-neh **moot**-tair

2. mein Vater
myn fah-tair

3. meine Schwester
my-neh **shvess**-tair

4. mein Bruder
myn broo-dair

This is my   1. Mother   2. Father
           3. Sister   4. Brother

How old are you?   I am _____ years old.

I'm allergic to nuts/eggs.

I love you.

What's for breakfast?   1. Cereal

2. Toast
tohst

3. Eier
eye-air

2. Toast   3. Eggs

11

It's time for lunch. I want. . . 1. a sandwich

2. Joghurt
yohk-urt

3. einen Hamburger
eye-nen **hem**-boor-ger

2. Yogurt   3. Hamburger

I'm hungry! What's for dinner?

14

1. Huhn?
hoon

2. Fisch?
fish

3. Pizza?
pih-tzah

1. Chicken?   2. Fish?   3. Pizza?

What's for dessert?

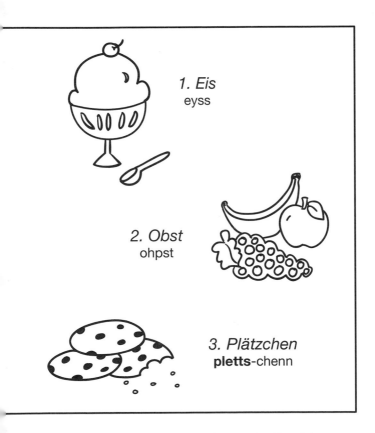

1. Eis
eyss

2. Obst
ohpst

3. Plätzchen
pletts-chenn

1. Ice cream　　2. Fruit　　3. Cookies

17

I like to . . .   1. Read   2. Dance

4. fahrrad fahren
fahr-raht **fahr**-enn

3. zeichnen
tsych-nenn

3. Draw   4. Bike

1. I'm sorry.　　2. Don't worry.

3. It's okay.

Can you help me, please? I'm lost.

Frohe Weihnachten!

froh-eh **vy**-nahkh-tenn

Merry Christmas!

Glückliches neues Jahr!

glook-lich-ess noy-ess yahr

Happy New Year!

This is delicious! I'd like some more.

Where are you from?   I am from _____.

die Tage der Woche

dee **tah**-geh dair **vaw**-keh

Monday *Montag*
mohn-tahk

Tuesday *Dienstag*
deens-tahk

Wednesday *Mittwoch*
mitt-vawch

Days of the week

Thursday *Donnerstag*
dunn-airs-tahk

Friday *Freitag*
fry-tahk

Saturday *Samstag*
zahmss-tahk

Sunday *Sonntag*
zunn-tahk

die Monate
dee **moh**-nah-teh

January

Januar
yahnn-oo-arr

February

Februar
fay-broo-arr

March

März
mehrts

April

April
ah-**prill**

May

Mai
my

June

Juni
yoo-nee

Months

Juli
yoo-lee

August
ow-**goost**

September
sepp-**temm**-bair

Oktober
awk-**toh**-bair

November
no-**vemm**-bair

Dezember
day-**tsemm**-bair

die Nummern
dee **noom**-airn

eins
eynss

zwei
zwye

drei
dry

vier
feer

fünf
foonff

Numbers

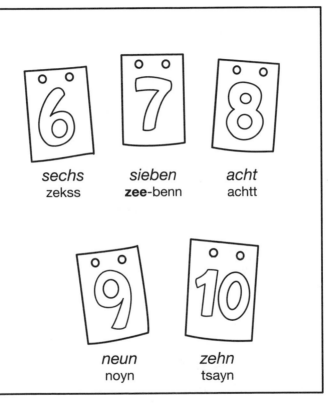

sechs
zekss

sieben
zee-benn

acht
achtt

neun
noyn

zehn
tsayn

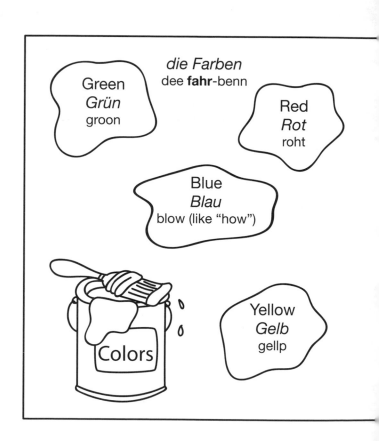

die Farben
dee **fahr**-benn

Green
Grün
groon

Red
Rot
roht

Blue
Blau
blow (like "how")

Colors

Yellow
Gelb
gellp

Colors

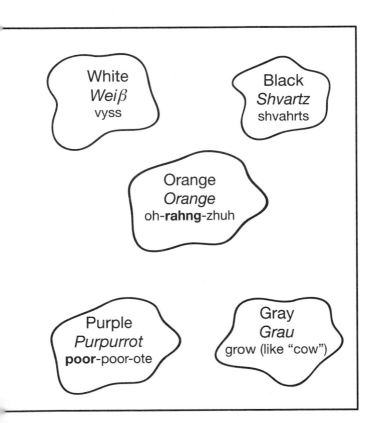

White
Weiβ
vyss

Black
Shvartz
shvahrts

Orange
Orange
oh-**rahng**-zhuh

Purple
Purpurrot
poor-poor-ote

Gray
Grau
grow (like "cow")

33

1. Let's go to the park!
2. Awesome idea!

1. How much does it cost?

2. It's one dollar.

Let's go to the beach! I will get . . .

1. *einen Badeanzug*
eye-nenn **bah**-deh-**ahn**-tsook

2. *Lotion*
loh-tsee-own

3. *ein Handtuch*
eyn **hahnt**-tooch

1. my bathing suit   2. my lotion   3. my towel

Please.

38

Thank you.   You're welcome.

It's raining. I'm taking . . .

1. my umbrella   2. my raincoat

Could you speak more slowly?

It's hot today. I'll wear . . .

1. ein T-Shirt
eyn tee-shirt

2. eine kurze Hose
eye-neh **koor**-tseh **hoh**-zeh

3. Sandalen
zahn-**dahl**-enn

1. a T-shirt   2. shorts   3. sandals

It's snowing! I need . . .

1. einen Schal
eye-nenn **shahll**

2. Handschuhe
hahnnt-shoo-eh

3. Stiefel
shtee-fell

4. einen Mantel
eye-nenn **mahn**-tell

1. my scarf   2. my gloves
3. my boots   4. my coat

I'm cold. I need . . .

1. einen Pullover
eye-nen puhl-**oh**-ver

2. eine Decke
eye-ne **deck**-eh

3. eine Jacke
eye-ne **yah**-keh

1. a sweater   2. a blanket   3. a jacket

Do you speak English?

Sorry, I don't understand.

I'm thirsty. I want . . .

1. *Wasser*
   vah-sair

2. *Saft*
   zahftt

3. *Milch*
   milkh

1. water   2. juice   3. milk

Excuse me. Where is the nearest . . .

1. das näheste Restaurant?
dahss **nay**-ess-teh ress-toh-**rahnn**

2. die näheste Bushaltestelle?
dee **nay**-ess-teh **buss**-hahl-teh-**stell**-eh?

3. die näheste U-Bahn?
dee **nay**-ess-teh **oo**-bahnn

1. restaurant?   2. bus stop?
3. subway?

53

Do you have a pet?   I have . . .

*1. einen
Hund*
eye-nen
hoondt

*2. eine
Katze*
eye-neh
kaht-zeh

3. einen Fisch
eye-nen fish

4. einen Vogel
eye-nen **foh**-gell

5. einen Hamster
eye-nen **hamm**-stair

1. a dog   2. a cat   3. a fish
4. a bird   5. a hamster

Happy birthday! My birthday is in

_____.

Can I . . . 1. Watch TV?
      2. Go to a movie?
      3. Go outside?

Where is the bathroom?

1. *Oma*
oh-mah

2. *Opa*
oh-pah

3. *Tante*
tahnt-teh

4. *Onkel*
unn-kell

5. *Cousine*
koo-**zee**-neh

6. *Cousin*
koo-**zann**

1. Grandma
2. Grandpa
3. Aunt
4. Uncle
5. Cousin (girl)
6. Cousin (boy)

I don't feel well. My . . . 1. throat   2. head
                          3. stomach . . . (hurts)

I'm tired. Time for bed.

Good night.